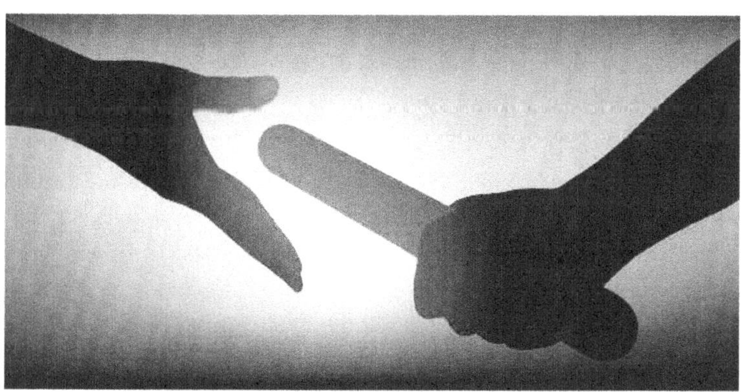

PASTORAL TRANSITIONS

A SEAMLESS HAND OFF OF LEADERSHIP

Dr. Gary Smith

Title: Pastoral Transitions

A Seamless Hand Off of Leadership

Author: Dr. Gary Smith

ISBN: 978-1-7330412-4-9

Published by: Engedi Publishing LLC, in the United States of America

www.engedipublishing.com

DEDICATION

This book is dedicated to my bride, Sandy.

She has been my best friend, my partner in marriage, family and ministry. This transition and book would not have been possible without her love and support.

I also want to dedicate this book to the incredible people of Fielder Church in Arlington, Texas. For 25 years, they allowed me to grow as a leader and seek God's leadership in "new ways of doing church." They are the real heroes of this transition.

TABLE OF CONTENTS

INTRODUCTION

INTRODUCTION

The 2008 Summer Olympics was filled with anticipation; the track events would be the highlight of fourteen days of intense competition. While the 100-meter race would determine the "world's fastest human," as usual the signature event would be the 4x100-meter relay race. This contest would determine which country was the best in the sprint races overall. While everyone knew Usain Bolt of Jamaica was the fastest, the relay race would stand out because it spoke of speed, coordination, and team depth.

For years the USA dominated this race. The 2008 team, made up of four sleek, well-conditioned sprinters seemed poised to repeat. They had been unbeatable in all of their meets prior to the Olympics.

Everything went according to form in the preliminary races as the US team came close to a world record. There was almost a "why not give them the medal and go home" mentality each time a qualifying race was run. The only issue to be settled was if this would be another world record-setting time for the Americans.

What would a victory mean to these men? They would forever be known as world champs. That gold medal would be in a prominent place at their houses to remind them of the great life-long accomplishment. Forever they would be known for winning the race that determined who was the fastest team in the world. They would gather on the award stand and hear the national anthem played to recognize who they were and what they had accomplished.

Yet the unthinkable happened when Darvis Patton and Tyson Gay fumbled the exchange between the third and fourth legs. For the USA, the race was over. Instead of victory and celebration, the moment would forever be remembered as another "what could have been."

Consider what this must have felt like to those four men—years of training wasted. All the "good try" and "you're still the best" attempts to reassure them couldn't come close to erasing their disappointment. Every time they would see replays of the race, they'd relive the loss. Their names would be associated with "the drop."

Just so, a dropped baton often becomes the legacy of a church when the pastoral transition is handled poorly. What could have been a glorious move forward for the church is often a step backward; many don't recover.

The often convoluted process moves at a snail's pace: resignations, farewell receptions, electing search committees, interim pastors, the mystery surrounding the interviewing process for the new guy, the "try-out" weekend for the pastoral candidate, the honeymoon period, staff turnover, new visioning for the church...all this usually leads to reduced attendance, declining ministry, uncertainty about the future, and division within the congregation.

Could there be a better way? For healthy churches with healthy leaders, would God have a process that does something new and different? Is it possible this is not a time for a step backward, but an opportunity for all involved to be blessed and the kingdom of God to advance?

How about the former pastor cheering on the new leader and spending his leadership capital to give the new pastor the greatest opportunity for success?

Could the church avoid the "leadership vacuum" that the enemy often uses to his advantage?

Could this be a time of growth and maturation of the vision rather than seeing so much that has been accomplished go by the wayside?

Is it possible for the new pastor to feel affirmed and supported by the outgoing pastor in a way that brings unity to the church?

Could the former pastor be happy in seeing his successor succeed? Could his greatest accomplishment be positioning the church to thrive after he's gone?

Is it possible the seamless transition between leaders releases the church to move forward in a way that impacts the community?

This book is not a foolproof way to make sure it all goes well. It simply chronicles how one church and two pastors made the transition of leadership and how all concerned—the former pastor and his wife, the new pastor and his wife, the church, and the community—were able to move forward in love, unity, and power for the sake of God's kingdom.

You will see there is no one-size-fits-all approach. Each church and leader have to find God's way for their situation. Even so, there are some basic principles to be employed no matter what the circumstances. Wherever these principles are neglected, the possibility of "the drop" is raised.

We will also see that only healthy churches with healthy leaders should attempt this. Honestly, if your church is unhealthy or you as a leader don't have the spiritual and emotional capacity to see this through, you'd be better off if you just resigned and let the Holy Spirit find the next leader who can bring the necessary healing to the church. If the outgoing leader does not feel a seamless leadership process is his last hill to climb, he is not prepared to lead the transition well.

Certainly, I'm convinced that God has a plan He wants to bless and let His people see Him work as never before.

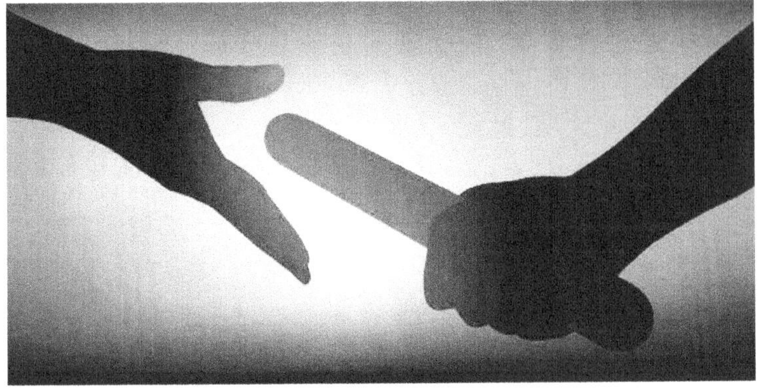

CHAPTER 1

PASSING THE BATON

CHAPTER 1

PASSING THE BATON

"We have to remember we are all interim pastors"

In a 400-meter relay, the talent of the runners amounts to little if they cannot hand off the baton at full speed. Before the event, each athlete must prepare for every moment leading up to the change in runners, knowing that, if it is not executed well, the whole team may lose. In other words, transitions matter. This is especially true when it comes to transitions in church leadership and more often than not, the baton gets dropped.

Charles served his church for 20+ years of very fruitful ministry. The church grew tenfold and became a leader in evangelism and missions. Their denomination considered them a model for ministry as they led statistically in mission giving and baptisms.

The congregation loved Charles and his family because they so represented Christ in the community. The feeling was mutual. After retirement, Charles fully intended to stay in town and be an active member of the church. He did not plan for a new ministry position and was unsure of the best way to hand off leadership.

Since he had never seen another way of doing it, he decided to resign and allow the leadership of the church to find a new pastor. God had richly blessed his years of ministry, and he assumed they would seek someone that would build on his foundation. Little did he realize, however, there were some in the church that felt the more contemporary music did not suit their taste and would seek a new pastor who would reverse that change. The generational conflict in worship styles would surface during this interim period and lead the pastor search committee to get someone who would reinforce their traditional music preferences.

The new pastor was a good communicator and quickly created a more traditional style of worship and ministry. As a result, the mood and atmosphere of the congregation completely changed. Traditional elements, which included dress, music style and focus were reintroduced. However, unlike Charles, the pastor seemed more interested in preaching "the program" than Biblical exposition. This culminated with the resignation of a very popular music minister as well several other staff members.

Over time, the church declined in attendance and evangelism. While it still maintained a sizeable core, the momentum of the church was lost and the vision significantly changed. Finances suffered and mission giving was curtailed.

Charles lamented this loss of direction and wished he

had examined another way. One in which the church could maintain its forward movement with a seamless transition to their new leader. All the leadership lessons he had accumulated would have been used as well to help the new pastor continue the dynamic direction of the church. Done properly, his transition could have been the most lasting accomplishment of his tenure as pastor. Instead, much of his life's work was compromised.

This experience points out how the process many congregations use for selecting a new pastor can actually set the church back in ways from which it may never recover. In this case, the interim time created a leadership vacuum that enabled certain members to redirect the momentum and vision in a destructive way. However, a closer examination of the situation, in light of God's Word, might have saved Charles and the church from this future.

Though Scripture gives no specific mention of choosing a new pastor, it is sufficient to equip us for every good work (see 2 Timothy 3:16-17). There are principles woven throughout the Old and New Testaments that help us see the heart of God in seasons of leadership change. Moses commissioned Joshua (Numbers 27:12-23), Elijah entrusted God's work to Elisha (2 Kings 2:1-25), David handed Israel over to Solomon (1 Kings 1:1-53), Paul charged Timothy to "guard the good deposit" that was entrusted to him (2 Timothy 1:14). In addition, we stand in a long line of faithful believers who have modeled how to transition a church well. On the other hand, we have also picked up some bad habits over time that make this difficult.

The roots of the church in America are primarily rural. Usually a strong lay leadership gave the congregation stability and was the basis for forming a lay team, elder board, or search committee to replace the pastor. This, however, prevented the outgoing pastor from being directly involved in the selection process, and very often the search committee had too little organizational experience to know how to find the right leader. Even those who had experience finding employees in the workplace struggled carrying this out within a fully democratic entity like a church. The process was also hindered by the committee's limited knowledge of the new pastor and his compatibility with the congregation. These habits can still hinder us today regardless of current resources.

Though there are ample background checks, personality tests, resumes, references, questionnaires, interviews, looking at past successes, etc., none can replace the experience of knowing the new leader over several years. This allows the congregation to see him in leadership, watch him in the community and follow the vision he has helped develop within the church. Even an unhealthy leader is able to give one or two good interviews.

No matter how many sermons the committee reviews, they will never know how he leads under pressure. And, because of the amount of change that takes place when a church transitions leadership, there will be pressure from the start. Whatever defect is lurking below the surface will be showcased within the first few months. If the church is unhealthy and led by the wrong leader, there is no process that will ease the pain of what needs to take place for the church to become what God wants it to be.

Some men, like Charles, leave churches they love having dropped the baton and finish their long-tenured leg of the race in regret. This should not be the case, and it doesn't have to be that way. Instead, imagine a different ending for Charles. One where he pastors a healthy church for many years and helps identify the best leader to take them forward. His congregation is able to both honor God's past faithfulness and believe that great days lie ahead. Imagine him walking out to his car after that final Sunday sermon full of gratitude. As the seatbelt clicks, he takes a deep sigh and smiles. He is excited for the church as well as the years of personal ministry in front of him.

Through biblical principles, personal experience, and the example of others, I will help you develop a plan to position your family and church for the best future possible. There will most certainly be bumps along the way, yet, by the grace of God, you will be able to hand off the baton at full speed one day. Be assured it will not happen by accident. The preparation must begin now.

CHAPTER 1
STUDY GUIDE

1 Has your church handled change of this magnitude successfully in the past?

2 Have the times the church has had interim pastors been a good experience?

3 Do you feel you have the leadership capital built up to lead the church in a new process for your transition?

4 Are you ready to make the necessary steps to ensure this new process can be completed, while maintaining church unity?

5 Are there leaders within the church who can give leadership for this type of new transition process?

CHAPTER 2

LAYING THE GROUNDWORK

CHAPTER 2

LAYING THE GROUNDWORK

"We will long be remembered more for how we left than what we did while there"

William knew his days as senior pastor were numbered and he began studying the best way to approach a transition. As was usual with other issues he had dealt with in his church, he spent much time designing a plan. This one would include elements of the books he had read, as well as, the example of other churches that had experienced seamless transitions. At last, he decided to present his plan to a key committee that had worked with him many times before with great success. This group of people, when the time was right, would oversee the transition of leadership within the church. To his surprise, nothing went as planned.

He was taken aback by how much opposition and rancor he encountered. He later discovered that an unhealthy staff member had been working behind the scenes to manipulate the transition process. This included false accusations aimed at William about financial impropriety, integrity, and denominational loyalty. Some even accused him of pre-selecting his successor and hiding his true motivations.

His lack of awareness with the church leadership led to a blow-up. In a matter of days, his resignation was requested. Even with twenty-five years of work and relationships on his side, William could not salvage this debacle. Those who opposed his leadership style had been working for some time to stack significant committees so they could control the transition to a new leader. He was simply not ready for that level of opposition. Few leaders are, and unfortunately, it happens far too often.

PRECLUDING THE PROBLEM

How could this have been avoided? Would it have been possible for William to foresee these obstacles and properly prepare for them? If some of these issues had been addressed much sooner, a successful transition could have happened.

Most experts on the subject agree that the success of pastoral transitions rests primarily on the outgoing pastor. His position and relationship with church leadership puts him in a very influential position that must be stewarded wisely. I have interviewed countless leaders who have been on both sides of the equation—the outgoing pastor as well as the incoming pastor. I have visited with many senior staff members that have watched the process. Some saw great success and others struggled through decisions that came close to splitting the church. I have also talked with lay leaders in various transition scenarios who led through seasons where the church developed and implemented new ways of doing things.

In all of these situations, there were numerous principles that paved the way to success. However, I am convinced that five, in particular, stand out above the rest. These components are crucial in avoiding major turmoil and potential disaster during the transition. In order to get the plan off the launch pad, it needs to possess the following five qualities:

1. **God's Will** – The outgoing pastor must know, with certainty, that the transition for him, the new leader, and the church is indeed God's will. This process has too many uncertainties and potential missteps for there to be any doubt. Along the way, unintended consequences will arise that could endanger the process and greatly harm the church. Emotions will go up and down like a roller coaster for both the pastor and his wife.

I have used this word picture to describe the range of emotions transitions like this can bring: Imagine your wife dating another man while you are still alive and discovering that she likes him a lot. Especially for the long-term leader, feelings will come that he never experienced before in his life. The only way to overcome them is by having confidence that this transition and new leader have been ordained by God. In doing this, he will be able to authentically invest in those who carry the baton forward.

The experience of Moses preparing Joshua to lead the nation shows how this principle can bless both the church and the leaders. Although disobedience caused Moses to drop the baton while reaching for the Promised Land, God clearly spoke to him of the succession plan to Joshua. Seeing this coming, Moses worked diligently to prepare Joshua for leadership.

Elijah did the same with Elisha. God put His hand on the new prophet and Elijah knew it. Just as with Moses, the transition was so clear that both men knew doing anything else would have been disobedient. Even when they encountered difficulties, they knew God had spoken and it led them to obey. How should pastors, then, position themselves today so that God's voice can be clearly heard?

The leader who is transitioning out must first devote as much time as necessary to hear from God on this issue. However long it takes and whatever spiritual activity is needed must be granted so that he can discern God's heart for him and the church. Fasting, prayer retreats, sabbaticals, discussions with his spouse, open communication with close friends and confidants, appropriate literature, wisdom from leaders who transitioned successfully, as well as, others who did not – these all must be a priority for the pastor that wants to see a good conclusion. When waters get choppy, God's words will anchor his heart.

John 12:7 says, "Many of the Jewish leaders missed Jesus because they did not want to lose their place." During this phase of discerning God's will, a pastor must see that he does not own "a place" as pastor of the church. Remember, because our life on earth will end one day, all pastors are interims. Embrace this reality because, unless Jesus comes soon, a transition will inevitably happen. God's will is good, acceptable and perfect (see Romans 12:2), and understanding this can help everyone deal with strong emotions and feelings along the journey.

2. Financial Security – The outgoing pastor must have a financial plan to provide for his family's future. At this stage of life, he is usually not burdened with the expense of children, college, and weddings. In fact, when it comes to income, this is a prime earning period. Because of this, however, many pastors end up hanging on too long because there is finally time to find financial freedom in ways they have not yet experienced before. Unlike other vocations, the pastorate does not have assets to be sold or stock to be cashed in to secure the future, and the lack of ongoing revenue streams can be frightening.

Therefore, the sooner the pastor engages a financial planner the better. A good planner can give accurate projections of what to expect during retirement years. This includes potential benefits, as well as, income needs during this time. While no one can predict setbacks in the economy, personal sickness, or death, a wise financial advisor can paint a clear picture of what will be needed in retirement and give tools to help prepare.

The area of finances can be particularly delicate in the transition. Each congregation is unique and must consider various aspects of their budget before making a decision. For example, a large church in the Midwest committed to a full salary for the outgoing pastor as long as he or his wife was alive. That is extremely rare, but it worked for their particular situation. Most of the time, a pastor will not receive from the church the necessary financial resources to completely meet his needs. As this will most likely be the first time in his life without a dependable income, a plan must be laid out so he can sleep at night that speaks well of the church and provides for God's shepherd.

This area has the potential to hurt an outgoing pastor and his wife. My best advice is to believe that anything given is a matter of grace. Comparing your church to what another church has done is fruitless and can only cause resentment. Later I am going to discuss the importance of the pastoral advocate, who will speak honestly to both him and the church about future financial arrangements. This is especially needed in cases where the pastor remains on staff.

Indeed, many churches decide to move the pastor into a different position on their team. This can, however, be fraught with great difficulty and used by the devil to fracture the church and hurt both leaders. Therefore, a clear understanding of expectations as well as the length of this agreement should be put in writing.

The pastor's wife is often more affected by a change in financial position than her husband, and her lack of confidence in this area can lead to much anxiety that can be communicated in the wrong places. Making sure she is part of the meetings with the financial planner is essential to her understanding of this chapter of their lives together.

3. **Marital Unity** – The outgoing pastor's wife plays a significant role in making a transition successful. Often her position of leadership has given her a deep sense of self-worth and fulfillment. Her grief during this period of transition could be as dramatic as her husband's. Like him, her role and place will be given to someone else.

The couple must approach this issue with candor and openness. Their willingness to express deep feelings is essential. Counseling sessions might be an avenue for this as transitions often pull out weaknesses in the marriage itself.

At other times, the wife wants to maintain her leadership role in the church, but this will only cause awkwardness and confusion for the new pastor and his wife. Humility will be paramount as she, too, is faced with taking her hands off the wheel. Many transitions have been greatly hampered because the emotions of the pastor's wife were not properly addressed. Her influence is second only to her husband and must be utilized for the success of the new leader.

The leadership of the church should ensure she feels recognized and appreciated. This gives everyone a wonderful opportunity to show the love and respect she deserves. Too many women labor diligently without any thanks from those within their congregation.

4. Future Ministry – The outgoing pastor needs clear direction for future ministry. He must not see this as an endpoint in his calling from God, but a recognition of moving to a new stage of what God has called him to do. Ephesians 2:10 says, "For we are His workmanship, created in Christ Jesus for good works, which God prepared beforehand, that we should walk in them." In short, there is still good work to be done.

A pastor should see his years of ministry experience as preparation for this next stage of his life. There is great potential for depression and regret if the leader does not have a ministry focus he is looking forward to at his point of departure. Though he may no longer be the senior leader of a church, God is not through with him yet. Later, I will discuss how a pastor can find his ministry sweet spot in the last stage of his calling from God.

The future should be an exciting season of ministry for the pastor and his wife. Without the responsibilities of leading a church, they can be free to work in areas that bring great fulfillment to their lives together.

5. Humility – The most important ingredient for a successful transition, by far, is humility. I have asked those on all sides—the outgoing pastor, incoming pastor, laymen, staff—and all agree: where there is humility, there is success and God is glorified. James 4:6 declares, "God resists the proud but gives grace to the humble." And, if ever there was a time when church leadership and God's people needed grace, it is during transition.

Where there is arrogance and ego, there will be disharmony and discord. Nothing destroys God's work in the kingdom like pride, yet true humility will display itself brighter in transition than any other trait. Each step along the way will require grace.

Any leader who thinks he can pull this off without God's grace will meet the devil face-to-face. There will most likely be unintended consequences that can throw everyone into a tailspin, and our only hope in those moments is the grace of God. Even gifted leaders who have navigated many turbulent waters will find themselves needing grace in this point in life more than any other.

"Have this mind among yourselves, which is yours in Christ Jesus, who, though he was in the form of God, did not count equality with God a thing to be grasped, but emptied himself, by taking the form of a servant, being born in the likeness of men. And being found in human form, he humbled himself by becoming obedient to the point of death, even death on a cross" (Philippians 2:5-8). With the mind of Christ, we too can model utmost humility. This transition process will need it at every juncture. When everyone involved chooses humility, God is glorified in ways that will leave a lasting impression on God's people.

Where any of these five qualities are not addressed, there will be great challenges, and missing any one of them can lead to failure. Focusing on four out of the five is not enough. While there are other important aspects to address in the next chapters, beginning with these is vital. Once the pastor and leaders are prepared, however, getting the church prepared organizationally will be the next hill to climb.

CHAPTER 2
STUDY GUIDE

1 What have you done (as Senior Pastor or leader) to spiritually prepare for this decision?

2 Does your pathway for determining God's will include something as radical as a change in process for leadership transition in your church?

3 Are you confident you can hear from God to lead your church through this process with a clear understanding this is God's will?

4 Are you certain enough to withstand the criticism from those who would say, "we've never done it this way before"?

CHAPTER 2

STUDY GUIDE

(continued)

5 As Pastor, is there a person you are confident in to help you with your financial plan for the future?

6 Do you and your wife have confidence in this person?

7 Is your wife fully on board with this decision as to how it will impact your financial future?

8 Do you have contingencies in case there are dramatic market changes that could impact your finances?

CHAPTER 3

CREATING THE STRUCTURE

CHAPTER 3

CREATING THE STRUCTURE

"The cardinal rule is there is no cardinal rule"

This church, the most prominent in the area, had a troubled history. Some doctrinal deviations had splintered it, and many wondered if they could survive. Frank became their pastor during this troubled period and a remarkable recovery occurred. Over the next two decades, this church grew to become one of the most mission-focused churches in the denomination and was a pioneer in planting churches.

The progress was not without casualties and opposition, but Frank stayed the course for twenty-five years and helped build a healthy church. When it finally came time for his transition, he announced that his departure would take effect once the new pastor had been chosen. Though Frank would not be leading this search, he would continue to pastor the church during the interim period.

In addition to this plan, he asked the newly formed committee to first consider his associate pastor. If they did not choose him, it would allow his family to begin searching for a lead role in another church. The entire process went smoothly. That is, until it came time for the congregation to vote.

They soon discovered the church bylaws required a 90% majority decision for electing a new pastor. This was problematic because, for many years, a small group of people opposed the changes Frank had implemented since becoming the senior pastor. These members campaigned to stop the election of the associate pastor and were almost successful. The first time it went to a vote, it failed. However, after discovering some of the votes were actually from non-members, a new one was taken and approved by 99% of the membership.

This process was successful because of the former pastor's willingness to stay during the interim period, thereby giving leadership when the process got off track. The result was an extremely smooth transition. Since that vote, the church has experienced continued growth and vision implementation, but it was nearly derailed because of the lack of organizational preparedness. When it comes to pastoral transitions, some churches will need to revisit their bylaws or risk becoming stuck in old patterns that no longer work.

This is why churches with a long history of "doing things the way we have always done them" have the greatest trouble with succession plans. In times past, these congregations had the financial clout and prestigious position that could attract the best of the best leaders with proven track records. The church seldom made a mistake in choosing a new leader, and always held the same predictable pattern of transition. The Senior Pastor would resign and the congregation would give his family a going away reception. A search committee would be formed soon after as an interim pastor stepped in to lead for a season. Eventually a candidate would be selected to be their new pastor.

However, most emerging leaders today would rather plant a church than deal with the baggage involved in changing a traditional congregation. Many older churches also wrongly believe that selecting a younger pastor will automatically reach young adults while simultaneously allowing them to maintain the heritage of their past. Members are unaware that the next generation approaches church with a new vision and process for reaching their peers. This has the potential to fracture the church dramatically. In these cases, the pattern for making transitions in the past is no longer consistently successful.

For this reason, it is helpful to develop a plan that includes someone with whom the church already trusts. This sort of leader gives instant credibility for the incoming pastor and can give him a clearer understanding of the church culture he is preparing to lead. It would be helpful at this point to examine the transitions in leadership we find in the Bible to gain insight. Although there is nothing in Scripture that specifically addresses pastoral succession, the few transitions that are recorded for us give guiding principles.

Unlike many of our situations, the majority of transitions found in the Old Testament, such as Moses to Joshua, Elijah to Elisha, or David to Solomon, were caused by the death of the leader. Because of this, they did not have to address many of the issues from the last chapter (i.e. finances, how the wife feels, does the leader stay in the church, etc.). However, when observing each case, a clear pattern emerges and applies directly to our circumstances today:

- God spoke to the leader about who their successor would be.
- God prepared the successor to take the mantel of leadership by allowing the former leader to invest in him.
- The successor patiently awaited God's timing to assume his position.
- The former leader made his successor known to everyone so that it was clear who they would follow.
- God then lifted up the successor in the eyes of the people.

There can also be adversaries to every succession. Though Israel knew Samuel to be God's anointed prophet and waited on him to anoint the new king, Saul opposed David's transition. At one point, even David's son Absalom tried to undermine God's clear choice of king. Disaster can sometimes come from unexpected places.

One of the great failures in succession happened when Solomon prepared to pass the baton. Many commentators believe the ultimate cause of the division that came to Israel began with the spiritual demise of Solomon. His last years were filled with immoral decisions and turning away from the God who had blessed him.

There is no substitute for a God-ordained plan. On the other hand, regardless of how clear the plan may be, if the church or leadership is unhealthy, it will most likely fail. Therefore, in order to avoid pitfalls and organize your church for success, there are several things to consider.

1. Avoid Manipulation – The leader must go to great lengths to ensure people that he is looking for the will of God. He must never appear to be manipulating the process. This requires that he carefully watch his motivations so as not to make it about himself, but the will and purpose of God for the church.

A man will be remembered more by how he leaves than all he has done before.

2. Adhere to the Church's Polity – A wise pastor will be knowledgeable about how pastoral selection works in his church. When opposition comes to the pastor, those who oppose will do one of three things: attack the leader, attack the process, or delay the process. This will be especially true in succession planning. Hence, the senior pastor should be more acquainted with the bylaws and processes of the church than anyone else.

One of the main reasons that planning must be done many years in advance is to prepare the polity of the church for new ways of selecting the next pastor. This is not manipulative, but wise foresight on behalf of the church and its leadership. The polity, no matter what it is, will ultimately dictate how the process is carried out. Here are some suggestions to consider for various church governments:

Deacon Led – In deacon-directed churches, the transition years can be quite difficult. Many churches rotate officers yearly which makes it challenging to have private discussions over a long period of time. I recommend that the pastor select 2-4 significant, trusted leaders to begin conversations about the transition. It must be stressed that these meetings and conversations be kept confidential. If the issue becomes public, it can significantly hinder success. Depending on the needs of the church and age of the pastor, the time frame for these discussions can range from months to years. For example, if the process of developing the next leader is going to take several years, this discussion can be often put on the back burner, but if the change is coming soon, it needs to be more focused and direct.

Elder Led – In elder-led churches, the transition years are easier. These congregations are accustomed to major decisions being discussed in a confidential manner without significant input from the congregation. Churches who are led with this style of leadership, can plan openly in their meetings without rumors or ideas being discussed with the general population of the church.

Council or Committee – During my transition as senior pastor, our church used a hybrid approach and formed a Pastor Advisory Council. This group worked with me to develop the long-term vision of the church. It was a rotating council with a 5-year term, and with possibility of a second term. This gave me a group with longevity, as well as, a place to have private conversations about issues of this magnitude. As a result, we had time to fully develop a plan to present to the congregation before it became common knowledge that we were discussing a transition process.

3. Consider the Options – There is more than one way to accomplish a smooth pastoral transition. By giving your leadership team time to research various plans, you will give them the opportunity to prepare the best solution possible. Though there is no perfect algorithm, there are a number of different approaches that churches have found to be successful in their context. To give you an idea, here are several models that have led to smooth transitions.

- The senior pastor announces his resignation, but it takes effect only after the new pastor is selected. In some cases, there is an additional period of 3-9 months that allows for the outgoing pastor to work alongside the new pastor.
- The associate pastor is promoted to senior pastor. This transition can be immediate or as long as 1-3 years. In this scenario, the former pastor will have no future leadership within the church.
- A co-pastor is hired with the full understanding of one day assuming the role of senior pastor. This is particularly popular among multi-site churches that have a number of lead campus pastors. The transition, in this case, could take many years to complete.
- The former senior pastor stays on staff to lead a portion of the ministry of the church. The new pastor takes clear leadership as senior pastor. This transition can be as many years as the church deems necessary.

Whatever the process, putting things in writing is essential. Sometimes, churches formalize this in what is known as a "separation agreement" that covers everything related to a future relationship, including salary, length of staff role, job description, office location, secretarial help, technical assistance, honorariums, ministry expenses, insurance, annuity payments, use of church facilities, etc. Clear documents that come out of open, honest communication will save a lot of hurt and misunderstanding. All the time and energy it will take to work out the little details will be worth it in the long run.

In succession plans, the cardinal rule is that there are no cardinal rules. As you put everything together and seek to implement it, there will be unexpected moments that surprise you. The following examples are quite common:

- No matter how foolproof the plan looks on paper, adjustments will need to be made. Make sure your process has good, regular communication so that you can make these changes without creating hard feelings. This is the most unpredictable experience in the life of a senior pastor. So, be flexible and ready to make adjustments.
- At times, it will get messy. If you combine the sinful parts of our heart with an experience that is complex and riddled with emotion, it's easy to see why. Once again, keeping communication lines open will go a long way.
- The timeline will change. Each process is typically longer or, in some cases, shorter than the church planned. The same is true of each stage of the process. Some parts of the transition might happen much faster than expected, while others take longer. Prepare to adjust the schedule as needed.
- Your plan has blind spots. Having wise counsel, from an outside party, that brings insight throughout the transition is a good idea. Though they might not always be right, having these extra set of eyes will help you identify potential pitfalls. It will also build confidence in the process when someone with "a dog in the hunt" looks at it with you.
- As long as either couple is alive, you will still be in the process. It is not finished when your succession timeline is complete.

CHAPTER 3
STUDY GUIDE

1. As pastor, do you understand clearly the process that is outlined in the church by-laws?

2. Is the current polity adaptable to a new process?

3. Will you be judged as "manipulative" by recommending a new process?

4. Are there leaders within the church who have the leadership clout to help the pastor see this through?

5. Have you identified those who would oppose this process and sought their support?

6. Is there time to be able to change the current by-laws so a new transition process can be approved?

CHAPTER 4

EMBRACING THE EMOTIONS

CHAPTER 4

EMBRACING THE EMOTIONS

"This process is like watching you wife date someone else while you are still alive"

This longtime, leading church in the denomination had a history that was widely known. The pastors were frequent speakers at any event within the denomination. In one of the most important cities in the denomination, this was by far the most prominent. Anyone would covet this opportunity to be the "next guy." At least it looked like that on the surface. From the beginning, the transitions, all of them, were failures of the highest magnitude. As a result of the church's position and exposure, everyone knew what was happening, or at least thought they knew what was happening.

The outgoing pastor was clearly at an age when transitions happened. With great forethought and planning, the church called a co-pastor who would assume the reigns.

Due to his stature and ability as a speaker and leader this would happen quickly as the two men began by sharing preaching and staff administration. Yes, "the best laid plans of man" are just that, plans by men.

Very soon it started to fall apart. The first thing that happened was the outgoing pastor got a "second wind" and began to second-guess the speed of the transition. He started to think. "I may have a few more years left in me." He thought the new man would not resent his getting back in the game to a greater extent than previously anticipated.

The next problem, the one that took the next guy down as well, was how the pastor's wife related to these "new guys." This was not only her husband's church, but her's as well. With her political clout she proceeded to undermine the direction of the church and the new pastor as well. This continued on with each succeeding pastor until her death.

When it was finally over, two great leaders had stepped aside from this transition. One found very fruitful ministry in the next stage and one left with a broken marriage and ministry. This church became the poster child for not doing it a new way. Their failure caused many to decide this was not a good way without realizing people who did not keep their focus on the main thing, the kingdom of God, will fail no matter how good something looks on paper.

All that has been written and said about this issue comes to the same conclusion: Most of the success of a pastoral transition rises and falls on the shoulders of the outgoing pastor. Certainly, this is not universally true. I could chronicle occasions where it was not his doing and the former pastor was not the reason a transition imploded, but most of the trouble comes from his handling of the process.

(Only Jesus handled it all perfectly, but even His followers had to be corrected along the way.)

In this chapter I want to deal with the emotions and feelings of the outgoing pastor. If he can "find God" and get it right, it will go a long way toward a successful transition. I want to remind pastors who are attempting this of a principle I have found to be very true: you will be remembered more by how you left than what you did while you were there. Sobering isn't it?

An example in the athletic world is Bret Farve, the Hall of Fame, all-pro quarterback of the Green Bay Packers. Few have been more successful at his trade than Bret, but how do you remember him? He leaves under a cloud as he goes to another team to "do it one more time" and show the world he still "has it". This experience includes several retirement press conferences as he fades from view while trying to the 'get back in the game" one more time.

How could it have been different? How about becoming a mentor to the new quarterback and enjoying the success he feels as his replacement builds on the foundation he established? He could have been the guy on the sideline holding the clipboard while this guy takes the glory, but also the "hits". It could have been one retirement press conference, applauded by his protégé and the organization, as well as, street next to the stadium named after him as he is adored by fans for the rest of his life.

It is sobering to know your days as senior pastor are gone. You feel you are becoming irrelevant as another takes your place. In the future, you might even have to do something you have never done. I know that this can all be difficult, but the time comes for everyone.

We are all interim pastors.

Here are several reasons that transitions bring about painful emotions:

- Much of our self-worth is tied to being a pastor
- It goes faster than we want it to
- We fight feelings of being irrelevant or unnecessary
- We fear the inevitable conflict
- Our legacy could be tarnished by unintended consequences
- We know that it will be a rollercoaster
- We don't want to be judged by the success of the new guy

However, if we don't engage these thoughts and emotions, we risk creating a codependency that can hurt both the pastor and the church. One of the symptoms of this occurs when the pastor thinks, "I need the church more than it needs me." So, let's talk about what goes on inside of us during this transition and see if God can prepare us for something that could be one of the greatest accomplishments of our lives.

EMOTIONS

The best antidote to the range of emotions is knowing for certain that the plan is God's will. The evil one is the author of doubt and fears. He will seek to magnify every possible issue into a rehashing of whether God is truly in this transition process. So, as far as it is possible, all involved must be confident in the Lord's guidance. Romans 12:1-2 shows that the pathway to God's "good and pleasing will" begins with surrendering our lives to His plan.

The pastor and his wife must be one in heart and desire for God's will to be accomplished. Many times, it is a man's wife that will help heal his hurts, give him godly counsel and remind him this is what God has planned for their lives. Constant prayer together and approaching each moment with the promise of God's blessing is vital. While moving through the transition, both of them will experience emotions they did not know existed. This process puts pressure on their relationship and might even reveal weak links in their marriage.

There will also be times when our hearts are the heaviest, that no one can help us. The strongest marriage and relationship cannot replace the reality that we must all face our giants alone before God. In these moments, the best thing a couple can do for each other is offer prayer and supportive love.

This is also a time for a pastor to deal with his ego. A transition will often reveal more about us than we want to know. While pastoring can be ego-deflating at times, we are used to receiving accolades on a regular basis. In fact, if we are not careful, this recognition and appreciation can become an idol in our lives. Watching someone else get that applause can cause jealousy and envy to rise up as never before. John 12:43 states "many missed Jesus because they love the praise of man more than the praise of God." This is an easy trap to fall into, and it's not the only one.

Someone once said to me, "I have come to realize I love the church more than I love Jesus." A transition can reveal a pastor's lack of commitment to the kingdom of God. Matthew 6:33 tells us to "seek first the kingdom of God," but many times we distract ourselves with seeking our own kingdom. Before long, we end up building an organization that feeds our ego and desire for recognition rather than one that glorifies God.

When talking about Jesus, John the Baptist proclaimed, "He must increase, and I must decrease." This must be the posture of a pastor and a transition will reveal which Kingdom he is truly seeking. Without having an eternal perspective, it will become easy to get caught up in the petty differences and nuances of change.

We can let people's excitement about the new leadership be something that gnaws at our soul and can explode in some other place. You might think, "I want people to be happy about this change, but not too happy." Humility is often being humiliated for the glory of God. This type of "decreasing" may be something the pastor has never experienced before, and it will happen at many points along the journey.

Here are some little moments that can cause big emotions after the transition:

- when we sit in the audience at the first Christmas Eve service
- when we don't have a key to the building
- when people do something for the new guy they used to do for us
- when we clean out our office and the new pastor moves in
- when his name replaces ours on the sign and the website
- when your opinion means very little, if anything
- when you hear about a project that you initiated, but your name is not mentioned

- when you hear people bragging on the new pastor's preaching and leadership
- when you simply come to church, walk in, take a seat and worship like everyone else
- when you hear that another outgoing pastor gets blessed in his retirement package more than you did
- when you realize a period of your life has ended and will never be recaptured
- when the new pastor's wife is introduced as "the pastor's wife" and everyone applauds
- when he receives positions within the denomination that you used to hold

These are all opportunities to "decrease so that He might increase." Emotions will surface that are deep within your soul. Feelings that are sometimes ungodly, but present nonetheless. Tears will come at unexpected moments. This sense of loss can only be overcome with the assurance you have obeyed the Father. And now, more than ever before, you must trust in Him. If you do, prepare to lay in bed at night being satisfied that you have glorified God. To find your worth any other place will always disappoint, but the peace and blessing that comes from the grace of God will make your heart overflow.

CHAPTER 4
STUDY GUIDE

1. Does the outgoing pastor have leaders he will allow to speak into his life about the places he is emotionally vulnerable?

2. Would it be wise for the church to hire a former pastor who has experienced this kind of transition to coach the outgoing pastor as this process is carried forward?

3. Will the incoming pastor be made aware of the emotional impact this transaction is having on the former pastor and wife?

4. Are there clear, written guidelines to help them deal with these emotions?

5. Does the outgoing pastor and wife have friends outside the church that can help them process their emotions?

6. Will there be written guidelines as to how the incoming and outgoing pastors will relate to one another?

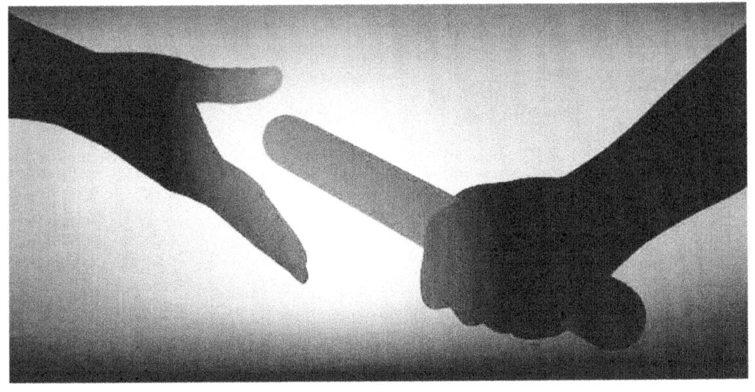

CHAPTER 5

FINDING AN ADVOCATE

CHAPTER 5

FINDING AN ADVOCATE

"...but for fear of the Pharisees they did not confess it, so they would not be put out of the synagogue, for they loved the praise of man more then the glory that comes from God"

– John 12:42-43"

Over time, Randy realized that his current church was not going to embrace his vision for leadership and direction. The many years of study, observation, and organizational frustration led him to start a church that reflected the biblical model he saw in Scripture. After much prayer, he left the prestigious position at his current church and launched one where he could be excited about serving every day.

The start was beyond expectations. Several hundred people believed in Randy's vision and showed up on day one. At the center was a group of elders who would oversee staffing and budgets while equipping the people for the work of ministry. This idea of an elder-led church was new to Randy's denomination, but it would soon become the model others pursued.

The church also reflected his heart for national revival. The congregation desired to see God do more than just what was happening in their town. God rewarded their faithfulness with waves of spiritual awakening within their church and across the nation. Randy quickly became a spokesman for revival throughout the world.

Over twenty years later, the fruit bears witness to a vision God had ordained and a leader who followed his soul no matter the cost. Multiple campuses, a heart for revival, and a shared ministry perspective has given unity and power to the church. Now, after a long season of prayer, Randy believes it is time for a leadership transition and the elders of the church agree who the new pastor should be. The new leader has emerged, over several years, as a man that believes in the direction of the church and can bring fresh vision to what has been established. It will be a win for everyone. However, there is a key player in the middle of it all that must first be identified.

Many factors contribute to the success of a pastoral transition, but few are as vital as "The Advocate." This layman or staff member, who is neither the new or old pastor, will speak into and help direct the transition process. He will understand each stage involved and can stand in the gap for the people affected. Finding the right man will take prayer and discernment.

Here are the nine characteristics every advocate must have:

1. Long-Term Perspective – This person sees the bigger picture of how a transition will bless the church and ultimately the kingdom of God. He also understands how the old ways of transition have often harmed the church and undercut the vision God has given.

2. **Relational Trust** – He has the "clout" to speak and, as a result of their confidence in his character and desire for the church, people listen. This does not mean he must be in charge of all the people and groups involved in the transition process. He simply carries enough weight that, when he acts, people want to follow.

3. **Pastoral Confidence** – Since he cares about everyone involved, he will be allowed to speak candidly to the pastors about the process. There will need to be many face-to-face, honest, and transparent discussions of very sensitive issues. So, both pastors must be confident that this person is looking out for their best interests, as well as the church's.

4. **Financial Integrity** – He possesses all the facts necessary for each group to make good decisions. The pastor has to be candid about financial circumstances so the advocate can represent him properly to those who will decide financial packages. This will also keep the outgoing pastor from being seen as self-serving.

5. **Leadership Dependability** – This person has the ear of the incoming pastor as well. The more confidence the new pastor has in this person the better the emotional and financial issues can be addressed. Where there is disconnect with this person, often there will be problems.

6. **Well Informed** – He knows facts and studies that will help during the transition. For example, the church who goes through the process of resignation, search, and

bringing in a new pastor will often see a 20% drop in attendance and giving. The advocate can speak to how this type of transition can be difficult on the outgoing pastor and wife, but it will result in a much lesser decline in future giving and attendance. If this was a business decision alone, the organization would see how the outgoing leader was working for the best of the entity. This will give the church much more freedom to do everything possible to bless the one who is leaving.

7. Honoring Mindset –The advocate is able to direct the "final Sunday" for the outgoing pastor. The pastor and his wife, therefore, can speak honestly about what they want for the weekend. While there will be many different ways the handoff might happen, having the right person lead this day is vital to a great celebration.

8. Rooted – He will be able to mediate any problems that might arise after the transition has taken place. His relationship with all parties as well as his knowledge of what was desired in every decision will greatly assist during these moments.

9. Compassionate – He is able to handle the emotional ups and downs of the outgoing pastor. When the grief of this process reaches down into his soul, the advocate will be the one he can weep beside. Being able to "vent" will also keep these emotions from overflowing into issues that can sabotage the transition. This person may also be one who has the candid discussion about whether or not the outgoing pastor should stay as a church member. This area is very sensitive and needs to be handled well so that no feelings will be hurt. Ultimately, this is a decision that rests with the new pastor. Whatever he decides must be done without a confrontation.

Where do you find someone like this? The answer can vary. In larger churches, many times this will be a staff member that has the respect of everyone involved. Executive Pastors, Administrators, Worship Leaders and many others have been excellent choices for congregations. Whereas, in smaller churches, the choice will often be a trusted lay person. It is usually better in these cases for the person to already have a place of leadership within the group or committee that will be making decisions during the transition.

As I have studied transitions of many different churches and leaders, the great value of this person cannot be exaggerated. Though he will work behind the scenes, the advocate might be the star when it all goes well.

How do you identify the person who is to be the advocate?

- Examine possible staff who you will allow to speak into your life as well as the church.
- Look for a person in the church who has the confidence of the people, but who, as pastor, you would allow to speak truthfully to you.
- Make sure this person will allow you to speak candidly to them about your financial needs, as well as how it best suits you to have the final handoff.
- This person must be a person who can articulate the process and details of the succession with various groups he will have to draw into this plan.
- Look for someone who will seek counsel from other churches and pastors as to how to structure the transition process.

The advocate must realize the importance of good communication as well as the need for confidentiality in all conversations with the outgoing and incoming pastors. This person will bear the brunt of criticism from those who will oppose any process that is new to the congregation. A failure in selecting both the process and the advocate will impact all concerned.

CHAPTER 5
STUDY GUIDE

1 Is there a clear choice within the staff or church to be the advocate?

2 Do people recognize the advocate person has the best interests of the church in mind?

3 Can the advocate person speak truth to both of the men without appearing to manipulate either?

4 Is there good communication between the person and the outgoing pastor?

5 Is there a need for a written document outlining guidelines for transitions and future relationship with outgoing pastor?

CHAPTER 5
STUDY GUIDE
(continued)

6 Is the outgoing pastor's wife willing to listen to what this person has to say?

7 Does this person have a clear picture of the finances of the church and the outgoing pastor?

8 Does he understand any tax liability that the outgoing pastor may incur with any severance benefit?

9 Can this person clearly shift his allegiance to the new pastor?

CHAPTER 6

POSITIONING THE NEW PASTOR

CHAPTER 6

POSITIONING THE NEW PASTOR

"The outgoing pastor must use his influence to "stock the refrigerator" for the new pastor"

Ronald came to this church at a very critical time in its life. The previous pastor had not given much leadership to the church and it had settled into a below average existence in an area that was rapidly growing. He had previously taught religion at a seminary and looked at the Sunday morning time like a classroom setting. Everyone in the church knew something needed to change. And Ronald gave them change.

In the early years things changed dramatically. This certainly produced lots of business meetings filled with debate and dissatisfaction. There were moments when Ronald thought he might not survive, but by conviction stayed the course. The growth in numbers and ministry impact was dramatic. Over twenty-five years later the church is one of the largest in the area and has an impact not only locally, but around the world.

The church had become a model that was duplicated in many other settings. The pastor developed an influence far beyond one church and his counsel is often sought. The style of ministry and organizational structure clearly produced the "church of the future." Even Ronald became surprised by the scope of influence he had achieved.

Since all pastors are interim pastors, eventually it was time for transition. Just as Ronald had given visionary leadership in those early years, it was natural for him to prepare the way for the next pastor. Ten years prior to the transition he searched out a co-pastor who would not only share his vision, but would be a likely candidate to succeed him.

The new pastor showed great patience to wait out this process and he had numerous opportunities to go other places. He purposed to learn from Ronald and so built a great relationship with him. They began to share leadership at various points to further pave the way for him to become the lead pastor.

This transition could be textbook for churches who have become multi-campus entities. While it was clear this man was the next pastor because he had worked at another campus, there were some nuances of this transition that needed to be addressed.

It was obvious to the church God had prepared him to be the next pastor and almost unanimously voted to call him as the new pastor. All the ingredients were in place: good communication, an advocate to help facilitate the details, and a written exit document clarifying all the issues that might arise. The transition proceeded almost flawlessly.

When the pastor determines it is God's will for this transition to take place, it must become his number one priority. As I've said, he will long be remembered more by how he left than what he did while he was there, and one of the best uses of his time will be to "stock the refrigerator" for his successor. The success of the new pastor is his success as well. So it is beneficial to give time and energy, in whatever way possible, to make this go well.

Since the outgoing pastor has more influence than anyone else, he is the most important player in the success of this process. There are many things that can occur that he cannot control, but he is best positioned to address most issues and bring them to a positive conclusion.

There may be no other season in the pastor's life where he will have this kind of opportunity. Many will not know all that he has done to make this transition successful. However, the pastor who shows humility will find these to be some of his greatest ministry moments. Scripture calls all of us to put the interest of others above our own (Philippians 2:3-4). This will be no more evident than when the pastor positions a new leader well for the future.

If you are the outgoing pastor, here are several moments to help set your new leader up for success:

1. Find ways to take a back seat in any gathering or event. Learn how to step back and allow the new pastor to step forward.

2. Look for any opportunity to honor the new pastor and meet his new programs or ministry efforts with great enthusiasm.

3. Never (and I really mean never) allow anyone to criticize the new pastor in your presence. This is just as important for your wife. A wrong look or expression can be seized by people as a license to become critical. Everyone must know they will have a fight on their hands if they talk negatively about the new pastor.

4. Use your influence to make changes today that will prepare the way for the next pastor tomorrow. For instance, six years prior to my leaving, I gathered the young members of our staff and asked them to describe the kind of church they hoped to lead. During the rest of my tenure, I used that meeting to set up good processes for the next pastor.

5. Get the staff shaped for the new leader. If you have been there long, the staff most likely suits your vision for the church. Therefore, you are the one who must go to these people and talk through a successful transition. In some cases this might even mean encouraging them to move their ministry to another place of service. You can also save the new pastor a lot of potential headaches by taking care of unnecessary or divisive staff members. No one else can have those difficult conversations as successfully as the outgoing pastor.

6. Change any organizational weaknesses. For example, constitutional shifts, staff restructuring, and budget priorities are a few of the areas you may address to help the new pastor have the best opportunity for a great start.

7. If for some reason the new pastor does not want you to stay in the congregation, this discussion should be held one-on-one and in private. Absolutely no one has to know why you no longer attend the church. The new pastor's desire, if applicable, should be enough for you to find

another place to worship each week.

8. Any church responsibility you have for the future should be decided by him. Only the two of you should know what was decided. In some cases, pastors want the former pastor to attend and even preach occasionally. This also allows you to show support for him. If there is a staff relationship that will exist, a very detailed written document must be established to prevent any misunderstanding in the future. If there ever comes a time when this is not working, this should be handled between the two of you. Again, no one should ever see anything negatively reflected on the new leader because of this change.

9. Give everyone some space. Most often it is helpful if you are gone for a period of time so that the new pastor can get established. My recommendation is 4-6 months. Some men stay distant for as long as a year. However long, it should be a determined time decided between the two pastors and not for public knowledge. It can even be part of the outgoing financial package for the pastor.

The outgoing pastor has to readjust his measure of success. In the past, he would see accomplishments that were tied directly to his leadership of God's church. But this all changes now. Sincerely rejoicing in the success of the new pastor and finding satisfaction in "setting the table" must be the places a pastor finds fulfillment in the years ahead.

This aspect of the transition is often the most neglected part, and the one that is the most difficult. There will be times the evil one will orchestrate new situations and question that could cause friction and division—

- What if the outgoing pastor is asked to be interim pastor at a nearby church?
- How about funerals and weddings when there is a need for both pastors to work together?
- How does the outgoing pastor handle any suggestions he may have about ministry needs and possibilities he sees that could help the new pastor's future?
- What if long-time staff members who have been close to the outgoing pastor want to discuss their future ministry opportunities and get his assistance in transitioning?
- How does outgoing pastor handle criticisms he encounters that could be helpful for the new pastor to hear?
- How does his wife handle past responsibilities and leadership positions that she may or may not need to step away from?

The outgoing pastor and wife will face some emotions and ministry decisions that have never encountered. In the past those decisions were usually about opportunities in ministry that would take them away from the present pastorate. This will be different now. There will always have to be a consideration of how this will impact the church they have just left, as well as the impact on the leadership of the new pastor.

Planning and preparing for this chapter of ministry will be new for the outgoing pastor. It is so important that he hears from the Lord and recognizes he still impacts the church he has left in many ways. He would be wise to seek counsel from the advocate, and other church leaders, that he knows will approach his needs, as well as , the needs of the church with wisdom and love.

CHAPTER 6
STUDY GUIDE

1. Is the outgoing pastor willing to do whatever it takes to ensure the success of the new pastor?

2. Does the outgoing pastor see the success of the new pastor as reflecting positively on his past leadership?

3. Does the outgoing pastor understand how impactful his presence is to the new pastor, either positively or negatively?

4. What are some concrete steps the outgoing pastor can take to help the new pastor's successful transition?

CHAPTER 6
STUDY GUIDE
(continued)

5 What changes can the outgoing pastor make before the new pastor arrives that will help in his successful transition?

6 Does the outgoing pastor have persons who will speak honestly to him if he is doing or saying something that is detrimental to the leadership of the new pastor?

7 Will there be a period of time the outgoing pastor will not be present so the new pastor may establish his leadership?
Who determines how long that will be?

8 Who determines if the outgoing pastor will stay in the church?

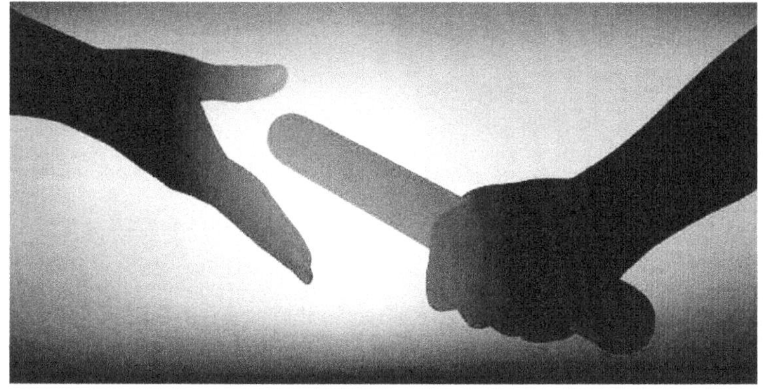

CHAPTER 7

MY STORY

CHAPTER 7

MY STORY

"If we let him go on like this, everyone will believe in him, and the Romans will come and take away both out place and nation"

— JOHN 11:48

Before I tell my story, I want to share another pertinent transition example.

Norman loved church planting. When others were settling into more predictable surroundings in traditional churches in the heart of the area where the denomination was strong, he felt called to go to one of those unreached cities that would be much more challenging. He located in a suburb of one of the largest cities in the Midwest and planted his life there. Over 28 years later a large church of over 2000 in attendance was thriving. His calling, dream, and hopes were fulfilled.

He recognized we are all interim pastors—even if we happen to be "the founding pastor." A time of transition comes to all of us. He was especially focused on keeping the vision alive and creating a seamless transition. His leadership position within the church gave him lots of chips to spend during this change in leadership. The church greatly trusted his judgment and understanding of what is needed in a pastor. They virtually allowed Norman to select the next leader with little interference.

The selection process went well as Norman found a man who had been a successful pastor and church builder. The new pastor was called, and a three-year transition process began. In those three years there would be a gradual transition of leadership between the two men. The first year was to be more of a get acquainted time for the new guy and the second year more directional leadership would take place.

Very soon Norman saw some major issues in the leadership style of the new pastor. While Norman had led the church by a consensus building leadership style, the new pastor was not good at listening to the ideas from others and came across as arrogant. This was more noticeable because it stood in clear contrast to the way Norman related to the leadership of the church.

The new pastor was not approachable and would not consider any ways other than his own. The crisis came to a head after the first year and Norman made the bold move to dismiss the new pastor. To his surprise, no one opposed the firing and the church moved on in unity to seek who would succeed Norman.

By God's grace, Norman saw that one of the satellite location pastors did have the leadership skills and style that the church loved. In just a few months he brought his name before the church and they overwhelmingly approved his promotion to be the next pastor. This transition went great and soon the church was moving toward the vision that had been so much a part of the past success. Since he already had a relationship with the new pastor, Norman and his wife remained in the church when he was not preaching at other churches.

My story, which began in 1991 at Fielder Church in Arlington, Texas, is unlike any of the previous stories. While the congregation had a successful past, it had plateaued in the previous five years and was about to experience great change over the next five. Being a very traditional Baptist church with a formal atmosphere, my leadership style (less formal, more innovative) further complicated this transition.

The previous pastor was a very gifted shepherd and evangelist, but his focus on buildings had also created a financial crisis that endangered the future of the church. With over 35% of the budget revenue swallowed up, the debt seemed almost insurmountable.

I sought to transform the face of the church, both in character and style, over the next five years. This included a complete changeover of the staff (23 of 24 positions were either eliminated or repurposed in the first 12 months). While these necessary changes brought about dramatic growth, they also caused many to oppose my leadership as well as the new direction of the church.

Even after the debt had been reorganized and our attendance tripled, there were those who simply didn't like the way I organized and led the church. Though the church became a national leader in growth and missions, I knew this group was waiting to "take it back." They looked for any leadership vacuum to appear so that the former days could be restored.

Around that time, I was asked to be the senior pastor of one of the most strategic and significant churches in Texas. Since I was exhausted from the battle for Fielder's future, I seriously considered it. In my heart, God was either repositioning my ministry or setting down roots for the rest of my life. The final decision came when God spoke clearly to me. Fielder Church was to be my home, not for the next 3-5 years, but for the next 20-25 years.

Since I was prepared for Fielder to be my last stop as a pastor, one issue that concerned me was how churches handled pastoral transitions. Usually there were long interim periods after the pastor left. If this would be the case, then my leaving would create the leadership vacuum of which others might take advantage. Therefore I knew my planning had to include a pastoral transition that would make sure the vision lived on beyond my leadership.

Early in my years at Fielder, I attended a denominational meeting called MegaMetro. We met to discuss specific issues that larger churches, like ours, faced in metro settings. During one of the side meetings, I heard a pastor tell of his transition from a long-term pastorate. I listened as he spoke of the seamless transition that happened in his church. In their case, the congregation called a former youth minister who shared the pastor's vision for the future. It blessed the church, honored the outgoing pastor, and set the stage for success for the new pastor. I catalogued that experience in my mind because that's exactly what I wanted for Fielder.

Over the next 20 years, we made many transitions to prepare our congregation for the future. Multiple worship styles provided an opportunity for the church to reach the variety of ages and music preferences within the city. Another dramatic shift came when we recognized the demographic transformation that was happening in our area. When my leadership started in 1991, the community of Arlington was 78% Caucasian. In 2017, it was 75% non-white.

In addition to this ethnic change, the city became younger as well. The shift within the church was again met with pockets of people that wanted to keep things as they were. As I began to see the coming transition, my desire for our church to flourish grew stronger. I also knew that, if people tried to return to the former days, it would soon die. Studies that were done of churches in ethnic-changing neighborhoods only confirmed this. As long as there was opposition within the church, none would be able to grow. I was of the opinion God did not want that, and I renewed my conviction to transition to a new leader well.

God confirmed this vision by bringing Jason Paredes to be on our staff. Little did I know, when he came to be our missions pastor, that he would have the dynamic preaching skills we discovered over the next three years. Both his ethnicity and vision perfectly matched what was needed for our church. It became obvious to all of us that Jason could be the leader to take Fielder into new places of ministry and outreach in the future.

I also had a conviction that the final decision was not mine to make. God's direction would be confirmed by the congregation. I made it clear to Jason that this was the case. I assured him, if God was in this, the church would embrace it and celebrate his promotion to Lead Pastor of Fielder. The direction was endorsed by the church in a 97.1% vote to call him as next pastor. After a two or three-year transition, he would be established as the new leader.

Looking back, my role in helping this happen came about in several ways.

1. Giving Jason preaching opportunities let the church see his incredible gifts in the pulpit. Multiple preaching venues enabled him to become a teaching pastor, as well as, leading our mission endeavors. This also allowed him to put vision in place for the direction he would be taking the church.

2. Elevating him to the senior leadership team allowed him to speak into decisions that would set the course for the future of Fielder. This also honed his leadership skills as he worked with various groups to move us forward.

3. Reorganizing our polity structure gave us the ability to have unhindered conversations about his transition. By the time the decision was made, the structure for this type of transition was already in place. We had established a pastor's advisory council that the church saw as a group of leaders who would give direction to this type of transition. The constitution and bylaws outlined this group as responsible for making recommendations for procedures if the office of pastor was vacated for any reason (death, resignation, dismissal). This structure made it possible for this committee to recommend a new process for pastoral succession.

4. The pastor's advisory council established a three-year transition process document for Jason to assume the new role as Lead Pastor, clearly outlining how the transition would take place.

5. Having numerous conversations with Jason about the

future gave me the opportunity to make staffing and budget changes before I left, setting up the direction he would take the church. Because the changes were in line with the direction I had hoped for Fielder's future, this further confirmed God's hand in the process.

6. After spending 6 months away, Jason asked me to be a part of Fielder's teaching team. Since my preaching and conversations wholeheartedly supported the direction of the church, everyone saw a unified vision from both of us. This greatly helped the transition.

One of the great blessings of this transition was getting to stay at Fielder. It has meant so much to us to still be a part of the lives of the people we love. All of these steps made the leadership transition seamless and our future possible. The church is vibrant and alive. Unity and vision have been preserved. And, by the grace of God, Fielder is positioned for a glorious future.

CHAPTER 8

PREPARING FOR FUTURE MINISTRY

CHAPTER 8

PREPARING FOR FUTURE MINISTRY

"We are God's workmanship, created in Christ Jesus for good works which God has prepared ahead of time so the we should walk in them"

— EPHESIANS 2:10

Mark knew this day was coming. He was excited to get "out from under" the pressure of pastoring. His church had been cutting edge in so many ways, but it only magnified the exhaustion he felt mentally, physically and emotionally. He knew he needed to get ready for the future, but didn't have the energy to work it through.

He also couldn't conceptualize what the future would hold. Would it be more of the same? Was being an interim pastor his destiny? Wouldn't that be more of the same? Would he go pastor a small church and focus on preaching rather than all the other "stuff" that goes with pastoring and dynamic church? He just decided to face the day when it finally arrived.

And arrive it did! Yes, there was the work of moving from his office. There were the many "honey do's" he promised his wife he would get done. Then there was the trip they had dreamed they would take that would be so wonderful. But the day came. That Monday morning he would wake up without a challenge or responsibility. No one needed him anymore. No office to go to and no meetings planned. He was lost!!

One of the greatest challenges for the outgoing pastor is deciding what to do next. The first Monday after his departure can be a stark realization of how much has really changed. Leaving behind a life's work will bring emotions and grief that he must prepare to face. Until this point, he has always known that another Sunday was coming and more leadership decisions awaited him on Monday morning. This is no longer the case, and it can cause a pastor to feel very empty. The lingering feelings of being "put out to pasture" can bring about discouragement and depression.

One disorienting feeling, for example, happens when the pastor has nowhere to "go" anymore. No office, no secretary, no required ministry to perform, no one depending on him, no calls asking for decisions, no schedule, no clear direction for the future...all of this can culminate in a loss of purpose.

A key part of successful transitions, therefore, is empowering the outgoing pastor for future ministry. Pastors who stop abruptly, without a definite plan for the future, fall prey to all kinds of difficult emotions. On the other hand, when a pastor has vision for what's next, there can be incredible excitement in his heart. One man put it to me this way, "Retire while you still have energy."

In the past, there were only a handful of options for outgoing pastors. Typically, this meant teaching at a seminary or being an interim pastor. While these types of opportunities are still great avenues for the outgoing pastor, only a few openings exist at any given time and are often followed by long periods of inactivity. How, then, can you invest in the lives of people?

Wasting the wisdom of a seasoned pastor who has gathered years of experience, is one of the greatest missed opportunities for young leaders in the church. In the Jewish world, many rabbis retire in their 50s in order to mentor and develop younger men to lead synagogues. It is simply assumed that an outgoing rabbi will equip the men of the next generation. This practice shows the great value in the knowledge and experience of older men. Sadly, most Christian denominations don't have the structure or thought process to help this happen.

I have come to believe retirement should not be in the vocabulary of the pastor. Finding ways to pass on wisdom to the next generation should be the focus of the outgoing pastor. But how can one do this? What are the best ways for pastors to invest into future leaders?

While there are a variety of pathways, a few principles and practices exist that can make this happen productively. If you are the outgoing pastor, consider doing these three things:

1. Spend a significant amount of time and energy working through the future in your head. In other words, this transition should never "sneak up on you." Do not wait until 8:00AM on the first Monday of your departure to start thinking about the future. A game-plan for this stage of life may be one of the most important programs you ever develop.

2. Create some distance in the beginning. Even when pastors stay on the church's staff in a different role, there must be a significant period of time that he spends away. The new pastor needs a season to assume his new role without the former pastor nearby. He needs to get out of town or go to a different church for a while. Do whatever is necessary to disconnect emotionally and physically for a temporary period.

3. Before transition, seek godly counsel about your preferred future. For example, one process I found particularly helpful was called "The 210 Project." It is based upon Ephesians 2:10, "For we are His workmanship, created in Christ Jesus for good works, which God prepared beforehand, that we should walk in them." Though it might not include being a pastor anymore, all of us have been shaped by God for a specific purpose.

Through survey questions, The 210 Project helped affirm my gifts and passion. This is what I would call a pastor's "sweet spot." Like a batter or golfer, the sweet spot is the place that provides the most energy and productivity. I believe every leader should go through a process like this in order to find the next place God has prepared for him. This could be the outgoing pastor's pathway for the rest of his days in ministry.

A pastor's sweet spot might include helping a struggling church for a season or leading a nonprofit organization. It could be a specialized place on the church staff that utilizes his unique gifts and abilities. For others, it may mean forming their own nonprofit in order to do the ministry God has called him to do. This may require some fundraising but would also enable him to invest into future leaders.

As the outgoing pastor, allow a small circle of wise friends and advisors to speak into this issue for your life. If you're married, start with your wife. She is your best counselor and can help keep you from any missteps. Here are a few other things to keep in mind:

1. Try some "low-cost probes" before you leave your present position. Those last months as pastor may provide you the freedom to explore future possibilities. This will also help you see what opportunities actually exist. Delving into these areas will also give you discernment as to God's direction for your life.

2. Do not make sudden life-changing moves unless you are certain it is your future. While we are much more portable than before, dramatic changes can get us in places that are more difficult to recover from. In other words, you might want to wait a few days before moving to Africa as a missionary at 65.

3. Discuss your plans with the incoming pastor. Since you may be doing ministry within the geographic area of the church, it would be wise to set boundaries for proximity to the church. This includes honest discussions about fundraising within the church if you plan to launch a new ministry.

Whatever happens in those early weeks and months, good preparation will go a long way. We all have to realize these changes are coming at a stage in life when a pastor's future years are much more limited.

CHAPTER 8
STUDY GUIDE

1. Will the outgoing pastor have the time to establish a new ministry focus for his future?

2. How does the outgoing pastor's new role in ministry impact the church?

3. Will the outgoing pastor have the freedom to raise money from church members personally to support his new ministry?

4. What office support can the outgoing pastor have as he engages new ministry opportunities?

5. Is his presence in the office a distraction?

CHAPTER 8
STUDY GUIDE
(continued)

6 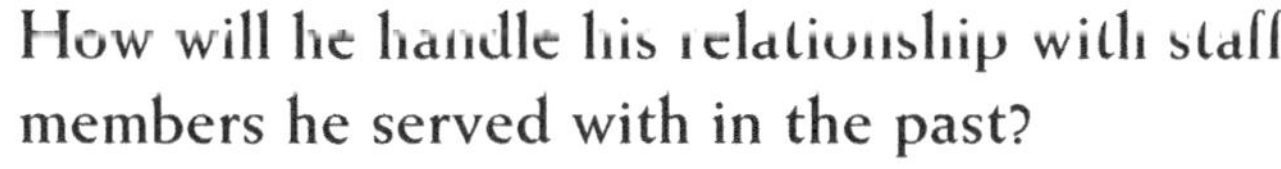
How will he handle his relationship with staff members he served with in the past?

7 How will the outgoing pastor handle any place of disagreement with the new pastor?

CHAPTER 9

UNHEALTHY CHURCHES BEWARE

CHAPTER 9

UNHEALTHY CHURCHES BEWARE

"Unhealthy churches should focus on getting healthy"

Tim had given his life to this church. While the church had not experienced great growth, it was well positioned within the denomination as a place of great expository preaching. This church was in the most prominent city in the state and was often looked upon for leadership. The church established a school that became one of the most successful in the southern United States and was copied by many. The pastor was greatly admired and became a leader throughout the denomination.

Yet, within the church there was a leadership group with an agenda. They had been caught up in a parachurch organization with great influence. Soon it became a "tail wagging the dog" situation as the group began to use their stature in the region where the church was located.

While the pastor agreed with most of the teachings of this group, the success of the organization and the school became dominant throughout the church. It also became a focus of those who wanted to pursue homeschooling as a way to educate their children. This leadership group became very powerful and dominant in the decisions made by the church body.

The pastor began to see this group's dominance was hurting the church dramatically. While they were well meaning in their heart, the parachurch was more important to them than the church.

The pastor decided this was more than he wanted to fight and resigned to enter a mission organization. While very few knew the real issue, it appeared this was just a transition to a final stage of ministry. No one realized this church was simply not healthy.

The leadership group positioned themselves so they would be very influential in choosing the next pastor. The person selected fit their profile: support for parachurch group, an expository preaching style, and a focus on homeschooling.

The problem came when the new pastor wanted to make changes that did not suit this group in many other areas including worship style, attire in the pulpit, evangelism focus, domination by this group in critical committees, etc. Soon the new pastor was being opposed by the same group that had "run off" the previous pastor. Battle after battle came because this group "talked a good talk" but really just wanted to be in charge. Eventually the church split and today this church has not only lost 70% of its attendance, and its influence in the community has suffered as well.

In hindsight, you could say the outgoing pastor could have fought to oppose this group. No one else had the leverage he had to possibly win the battle. Sadly, many men choose to leave rather than fight. This type of confrontation is very painful and can be devastating to a person's ministry. The sidelines are lined with men who attempted this but could not overcome the tremendous power some have within the church.

What does this tell us when it comes to pastoral transition? The health of the church is a major factor. Watching these transitions in other churches and attempting to duplicate them often misses a key factor: healthy churches can do healthy things, unhealthy churches can't.

What is a healthy church? That is another book to be written by other men, not me! But a wise leader who is seeking a new way to make pastoral transitions would be wise to do some leadership evaluations to see if this church has the capacity to attempt it.

Here are a few suggestions:

- What is the leadership stature of the present pastor? This means a willingness to honestly look at the "followship" of the church presently. A pastor must evaluate how his current leadership team feels about him and how willing they are to follow. If conflict has been constant in recent days, the outgoing pastor won't be able to lead the transition well.

- The pastor would be wise to privately speak with key leaders to assess his position within the church. While any change like this will have a measure of opposition, he needs to know the depth of those who want to lead the church away from his vision. If his vision for the future of the church has not been settled and accepted by the overwhelming majority, this change could be used to take the church backward.

- The pastor needs to know the position of his staff. If he does not have a loyal following in this group, he most likely does not have it within the church. Many churches who have attempted this type of transition have found there are those on the staff who have been secretly disloyal and this gives them an avenue to undermine the pastor.

- A leader needs to ask, "What is the change temperature?" of the congregation. This means he needs to assess how much change has been accepted before as a barometer for change in the future. If he has only attempted small adjustments previously, he could throw the church in turmoil by suggesting something so significant.

- A pastor might ask the question, "Am I ready to face this type of turmoil in my last days as pastor and see it through?" Certainly, the easiest way to end your ministry is to simply resign, have a going-out party and be everyone's hero. This transition can end differently and can taint a person's last days if it does not go right. A pastor must evaluate the potential for success as well as evaluating his capacity for the battle.

- Another critical question: "Is the pastor seen as a control guy who is just wanting to manipulate the process to get his way?" It is critical to this process that he affirms this is God's choice for the pastor of the future and this is affirmed within the congregation. Very few churches want the former pastor selecting the next leader without agreement with the congregation. This balance in decision making is healthy and speaks of a healthy church. I personally did not want the burden of making the choice on my own.

- It is essential that a pastor has the confidence of the leadership of the church. Those private conversations with the "movers and shakers" of the church cannot be overlooked. If this is a group that needs to be broken up, this usually cannot happen quickly, so the leaders must be willing to stay as long as it takes to get the church healthy.

This type of transition is not for the faint-hearted. If your self-worth is tied up in people's approval and you cannot stomach those who would fight this, it's best to simply resign and get on with your life in ministry. If you see the vision of a seamless transition that allows the church to make a step forward with a new leader, then pray a lot and give it a try and see what God says.

As one who has been on the good side of this and knows many who have done it as well, there may not be anything more satisfying and kingdom lifting than deciding "my time is up," and then leading the church to a new day and pastoral leadership.

CHAPTER 9
STUDY GUIDE

1. How will the outgoing pastor determine church health?

2. Does the church need to hire an outside group to help them understand the health of the church?

3. Are there staff members who will oppose this transition?

4. Are there church leaders who are waiting for chance to oppose any variance in transitions process?

5. Do those who have opposed the present pastor have the influence to significantly undermine the new process?

APPENDIX I

PASTORAL TRANSITION TRANSCRIPT

The following is a transcript from a presentation by Jason Paredes, incoming Pastor at Fielder Road Baptist Church. Dr Gary Smith is the outgoing Pastor in this transcript.

1. PROS AND CONS FROM THE INCOMING PASTOR'S PERSPECTIVE

Cons

You miss all the "new guy" momentum of pastoral exchange.

- A prophet is never welcome in his own hometown – "Isn't this guy just the Hispanic pastor?"
- You live under the shadow of the old pastor, especially if the church perceives he orchestrated the move – "It's not mine to give you."

It makes changing culture dicey.

- It's hard to talk about the need for change when the old pastor is in the room. Everything can feel like a dig.

- You have to constantly be sensitive to how he might hear it.
- It's easier when you can throw the old guy under the bus!

It makes the timing of grabbing the reigns tricky.

- When you come in as the new pastor, it's yours to own from day one.
- When it's a transition, you have to consider what to take and when, and when you just need to sit back and wait. (when do I own teaching team retreats? LT meetings? Planning retreats? Deacon meetings? - see process.

Pros

The number one win is pre-built relational equity – both in the church and in the community.

- People feel comfortable giving to someone they know and trust. – share about how our giving increased by 15% in year 1.
- Easy to get buy in for vision because it feels familiar even if it is radically different.
- The city recognizes a leader who's lived there for years.

You can hit the ground running in the office.

- My day #1 as lead pastor was my day 2,640 in the office. 11 years of history makes a difference!
- You know the rhythms, the relationships, the staff-dynamics.

It gives time and space for the incoming pastor to pray, dream, and plan, but not need to own anything yet.

- A year to solidify vision.
- Able to take the senior leadership team on the journey.
- Gives space to travel and visit other ministries.

The necessary changes can happen under the protection of the outgoing pastor. He plays his chips since he has so many more!

The mentorship relationship between outgoing and incoming pastor is much stronger because of an existing relationship.

- The outgoing pastor has deep history that is gold for the incoming pastor.
- He doesn't feel threatened to get advice if they are friends and partners in the ministry.

2. WHAT I NEEDED FROM THE OUTGOING LEADER

Constant encouragement – "you can do this!"

Room to fly – "you go ahead and take it."

Someone to deliver the role over to me.

- The church wanted to know what Gary thought about the transition. Was it forced? Was he behind it? Did he believe in me?
- His greatest word was, "Jason is going to be my pastor. I'll follow him anywhere!"

3. WHAT I NEEDED TO DO FOR THE OUTGOING LEADER

I needed to protect his reputation.

- The danger of Absalom – "If I were the king…"
- You need the attitude of David – "He is the Lord's anointed."
- Even when we have different opinions.

I needed to be sensitive to his feelings.

- "Someone else is dating my wife while I'm still alive."
- One person is giving everything up while the other is taking it!

I needed to make space for him in the long-term even after the transition.

- One of the healthiest signs for our church is the continuity.
- Gary is still a teaching pastor
- He is my #1 supporter. Why wouldn't I have him around?

4. MY STORY

I wanted to leave, but the Lord just wouldn't let me.

- Times of prayer and brokenness over Fielder.
- Call to be faithful even if I never became what I expected. "If I was a missions pastor for the rest of my life, but I was serving the Lord, would I be OK with that?"

First conversation at IHOP

- Call from a large church to go as a teaching pastor with a look to transition to lead pastor – 3 times the size of Fielder.
- Felt like the Lord telling me to stay – but I needed to know Gary's opinion.
- Not mine to give you, but I believe you could be the next person.
- I just found out he mentioned this to another staff person just a couple of years after I had come.
- I also needed to hear the process. Whose was it to give to me if that is what the Lord willed?
- The question of timing – trip to Preteen camp
- Am I needing this before you are ready to give it?

- The two of us had to get gut-level honest. The health of the church was at stake.
- The Lord called me to stay and he tested that call.
- Multiple more calls from other large churches.
- Came a moment when I said to Gary, "I'm anteing up. Is the church going to do the same?"
- It was an act of faith and a
- risk, but the Lord rewarded it.

5. LESSONS LEARNED

The transition had to be more about celebrating Gary than passing the reigns to me. No fanfare. Just picking up and leading on. Fasting and headache story.

There's a balance about when to take the reigns.

- Don't be afraid to take the reigns when it's time. – Gary always said, "I'd be worried if you didn't want to take over."
- Don't try to take the reigns too early. It's still his ship until the transition is over. Even then, it's still the Lord's and not mine!

Clear vision was the key to a healthy transition from my part.

- Gary had to hand me the ball, but I had to run with it.
- Vision helped me know where to run and gave people direction to follow.

Fasting and praying was my greatest form of leadership capital.

- I didn't have experience, tenure, or leadership clout.
- My chip count was low!
- Being a praying and fasting leader gave people confidence in my young leadership.

I had to get comfortable in my own skin.

- I am not Gary Smith. – He is woo. Everyone loves him. I'm prickly.
- I had to realize the church didn't need Gary Smith. They needed Jason Paredes…at least for now.
- Share about my time of prayer – I'm called to communicate the vision until people are sick of it and discipline us toward it.

6. WHAT I'D DO DIFFERENTLY IF I COULD DO IT OVER AGAIN

I'd read more, study more, and ask more questions.

I'd study myself more.

- I've had to self-discover way too much on the job, and the cost has been high for the team.
- The more I know about how I work, the more the team knows how to adjust around me.

I would have made more changes while I was under Gary's protection.

- I'd tip more cows and blame it on him!
- I'd have him play more chips for me.

7. HOW TO KNOW YOU ARE RIGHT FOR THIS TRANSITION

You have to hear it from God – I am God's man for this moment.

You have to hear it from staff – Curtis story – will they follow?

You have to hear it from the people – you need leadership buy in.

- Caution – don't take it too soon.
- Don't believe your own press. Momma's always going to believe in you!

Check for the right timing – is it the right time not just for you but for the outgoing pastor and the church? – preteen car conversation

Check for the clear vision – is God putting something on your heart, a burning passion to lead the church into the future? Not just a title?

Check for open hands – are you willing to step into this knowing it may not work? – Gary's words – "It's not mine to give you." – We might go through all of this and it can still fail.

APPENDIX I

APPENDIX II

NEXT STEPS

Ok? Where do I go from here? What are my first steps?

1. Spend the time necessary to hear from God personally. This cannot be short-changed or abbreviated in lieu of a quick decision. Just as Nehemiah went alone to survey the landscape and let God speak, you and only you can discover the mind of the Lord for your church.
2. Make ABSOLUTELY SURE your wife is COMPLETELY on board with this decision and the process. She has to be your partner in this process. She has to also know there are parts of this that may change. She also needs to identify her place in the future.
3. Read books, study other churches and find every resource you uncover to become the best informed person who sits at the table and with the most knowledge of this process.

4. Put together a one page action plan. This is not the final or an unchangeable document. It is just your first thoughts on the subject. Make sure you aren't going to be defensive when you begin to roll this out to leaders within your church.

5. Assess the health of the church. Has your church dealt with change well in the past? Are there any staff or lay leaders who would undermine this because of a broken relationship with you? What could you do in the near future to rectify these relationships?

6. Identify 2-5 leaders within your church who you can have a conversation with who will keep this in ABSOLUTE confidence. This must be people who are influencers within the church and will speak honestly to you about their feelings.

7. Together, with those leaders, devise a plan of action you and they would be willing to present to the church. At this point this must still be an absolutely confidential conversation.

8. Identify the person who will serve as the Advocate in this process.

9. Begin a process to bring this issue before the church. Start with influential groups. (personnel committee, deacon officers, deacons, finance committee, small group leaders)

10. Pray, pray, pray!

APPENDIX III

ACTION PLAN

What has God been telling you in your quiet time with Him?

How have discussions with your wife gone about what you are hearing from God?

How have discussions gone with your wife about this transition?

How is the health of your Church?

On a scale of 1-10 (with 1 being worst) how is the health of your Church?

1 2 3 4 5 6 7 8 9 10 (Circle One)

Are there any staff members who might undermine this transition?

Name:

Name:

Are there any lay leaders that might undermine this transition?

Name:

Name:

Who are the leaders in your Church that you can trust to discuss this with you?

Name:

Name:

What are the next steps to help your Church with this transition?

Step 1

Step 2

Step 3

Step 4

Step 5

What groups and when do you need to start discussing the transition plan?

Group:	Date:
Group:	Date:
Group:	Date:

What is God telling you about this process and plan as you continue with the process?

APPENDIX IV

RESOURCES AVAILABLE FOR FURTHER STUDY

Book: *Next: Pastoral Succession That Works* by William Vanderbloemen and Warren Bird

A book that explores the many ways churches have looked at succession for the Senior Pastor. This book explores the implications of the various ways churches have attempted to create a succession process. The book explores the reasons, so many churches have failed to transfer, trying new ways to transfer leadership.

https://www.lifeway.com/en/product/next-expanded and updated-ed-P0 08011849

www.210project.com

Website that contains the process for a pastor to find his "sweet spot" for his ministry in the future. Book to read, as well as tests to be taken that will assist the pastor in discovering his next stage of life and ministry.

The Healthy Church

(SBTC conference done by Jason Paredes and Gary Smith) Conference Jason Paredes and I did for the Southern Baptists of Texas Convention. We explored the nuances of our transition at Fielder Church.

https://training.sbtexas.com/onlinetraining/the-healthy-church-part-1/1184/

www.realchurchsolutions.com

Author's website for further help in exploring pastoral succession in your church. You can contact Dr. Smith at his email:

gsmith@realchurchsolutions.com

Made in the USA
Monee, IL
25 June 2020

33571073R10069